COMMAND PROMPT

LIST OF COMMAND PROMPT COMMANDS

KABIR DAS

Copyright © Kabir Das
All Rights Reserved.

ISBN 979-888555101-4

This book has been published with all efforts taken to make the material error-free after the consent of the author. However, the author and the publisher do not assume and hereby disclaim any liability to any party for any loss, damage, or disruption caused by errors or omissions, whether such errors or omissions result from negligence, accident, or any other cause.

While every effort has been made to avoid any mistake or omission, this publication is being sold on the condition and understanding that neither the author nor the publishers or printers would be liable in any manner to any person by reason of any mistake or omission in this publication or for any action taken or omitted to be taken or advice rendered or accepted on the basis of this work. For any defect in printing or binding the publishers will be liable only to replace the defective copy by another copy of this work then available.

Contents

1. Introduction To Cmd — 1
2. Windows Command Prompt (cmd) Commands — 5
3. Command Prompt(cmd) Commands — 26

CHAPTER ONE

INTRODUCTION TO CMD

CMD is an acronym for Command. Command prompt, or CMD, is the command-line interpreter of Windows operating systems. It is similar to Command.com used in DOS and Windows 9x systems called "MS-DOS Prompt". It is analogous to Unix Shells used on Unix like system. The command prompt is a native application of the Windows operating system and gives the user an option to perform operations using commands.

Command prompt makes use of the command-line interface to interact with the User. In the Windows operating system, this command prompt interface is implemented through the Win32 console. User can open the interface by via the CMD run command or by going to its original location **C:\Windows\system32\cmd.exe.**

Understanding CMD

With the command shell, you can have direct interaction with the operating system. Think command prompt as an interpreter that accepts the commands or the User's inputs and translate them into **machine language.** These commands are predefined and perform a specific task. These commands can be clubbed together as well to perform a series of task. Also, these commands need not be entered manually and can be written in a batch file to automate some of the manual tasks like taking a scheduled server backup, deleting junk files and so on. These commands are very handy at the time of network troubleshooting or for a day to day work. These commands can be called from many **programming languages such as Java,** which allows the programmer to perform task directly via the command prompt, which would otherwise take several code lines to be written essentially to perform the same task.

How to access CMD?

To access the command prompt irrespective of what version you are using, follow the below steps. One of the quickest ways to access the command prompt is to make use of Run Window. To open the run window, press the **Windows key + R** on your keyboard. Once you do, that run window will open and then write cmd and press enter.

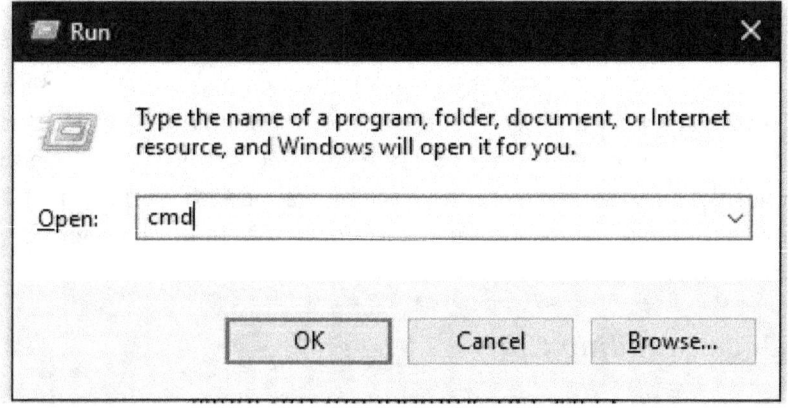

Windows key + R

As soon as you press the ok command prompt window will get open up.

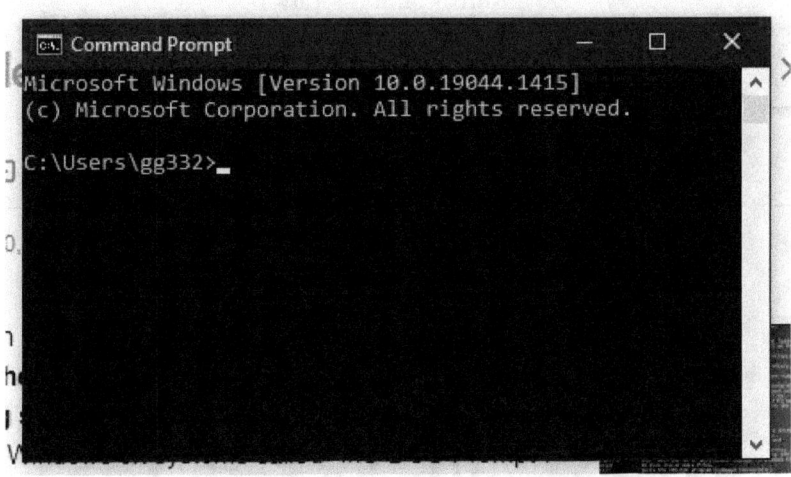

cmd or command prompt

To run the command prompt in the administration mode, type cmd in the search bar present in the taskbar, then right-click on cmd. You will see an option Run as administration click ok and then **command prompt** will open in the admin mode.

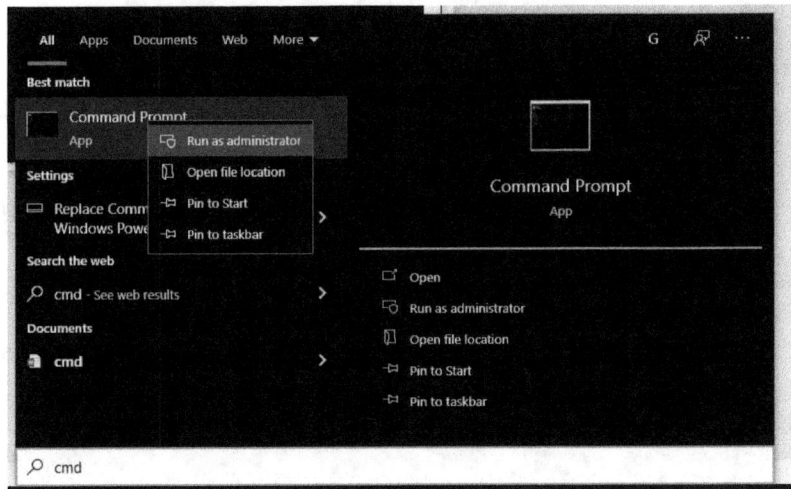

COMMAND PROMPT

Run as administration

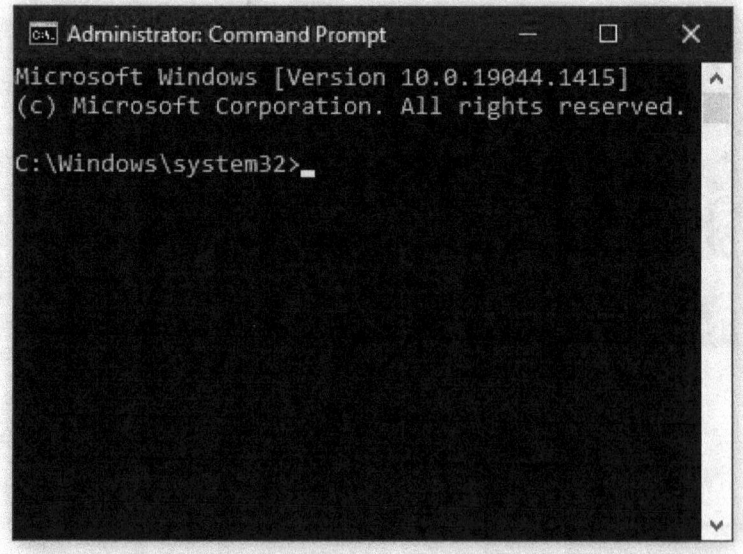

command prompt in admin mood

CHAPTER TWO

Windows Command Prompt (CMD) Commands

Windows Command Prompt Commands

- If you haven't poked around inside Windows' command line, you're missing out. There are lots of handy tools you can use if you know the correct things to type.

1. Assoc

```
C:\Windows\system32\cmd.exe
.xlsmhtml=excelmhtmlfile
.xlsx=Excel.Sheet.12
.xlt=Excel.Template.8
.xlthtml=Excelhtmltemplate
.xltm=Excel.TemplateMacroEnabled
.xltx=Excel.Template
.xlw=Excel.Workspace
.xlxml=Excelxmlss
.xm=VLC.xm
.xml=xmlfile
.xpm=IrfanView.xpm
.xrm-ms=MSSppLicenseFile
.xsl=xslfile
.xspf=VLC.xspf
.ZFSendToTarget=CLSID\{888DCA60-FC0A-11CF-8F0F-00C04FD7D062}
.zip=CompressedFolder

C:\Users\Tina>assoc.txt
.txt=txtfile
```

Assoc

Most files in Windows are associated with a specific program that is assigned to open the file by default. At times, remembering these associations can become confusing. You can remind yourself by entering the command **assoc** to display a full list of filename extensions and program associations.

You can also extend the command to change file associations. For example, **assoc .txt=** will change the file association for text files to whatever program you enter after the equal sign. The assoc command itself will reveal both the extension names and program names, which will help you properly use this command.

In Windows 10, you can view a more user-friendly interface that also lets you change file type associations on the spot. Head to **Settings (Windows + I) > Apps > Default apps > Choose default app by file type.**

2. Cipher

```
C:\Windows\system32\cmd.exe                    —    □    ×
C:\Users\Tina>cipher

Listing C:\Users\Tina\
New files added to this directory will not be encrypted.

U .cisco
U .mediathek3
U .sambox.cache
U 3D Objects
U Contacts
U Documents
U Downloads
U Dropbox
U Favorites
U Google Drive
U Links
U MediathekView
U Music
U OneDrive
```

Cipher

Deleting files on a mechanical hard drive doesn't really delete them at all. Instead, it marks the files as no longer accessible and the space they took up as free. The files remain recoverable until the system overwrites them with new data, which can take some time.

The cipher command, however, wipes a directory by writing random data to it. To wipe your C drive, for example, you'd use the **cipher /w:d** command, which will wipe free space on the drive. The command does not overwrite undeleted data, so you will not wipe out the files you need by running this command.

You can use a host of other cipher commands, however, they are generally redundant with BitLocker enabled versions of Windows.

3. Driverquery

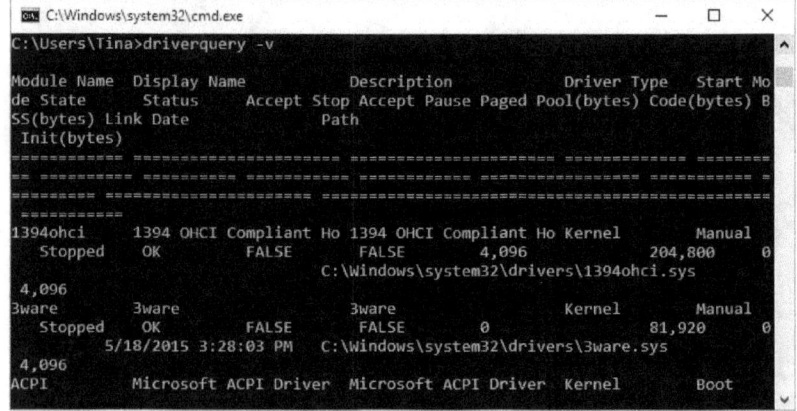

Driverquery

Drivers remain among the most important software installed on a PC. Improperly configured, missing, or old drivers in Windows can cause all sorts of trouble, so it's good to have access to a list of what's on your PC.

That's exactly what the **driverquery** command does. You can extend it to **driverquery -v** to obtain more information, including the directory in which the driver is installed.

4. File Compare

```
C:\Windows\system32\cmd.exe                                    —    □    ×

C:\Users\Tina>fc /C "C:\Users\Tina\Documents\Example 1.txt" "C:\Users\Tina\Docume
nts\Example 2.txt"
Comparing files C:\USERS\TINA\DOCUMENTS\Example 1.txt and C:\USERS\TINA\DOCUMENTS
\EXAMPLE 2.TXT
***** C:\USERS\TINA\DOCUMENTS\Example 1.txt
This line is identical.
This is EXAMPLE File 1.
***** C:\USERS\TINA\DOCUMENTS\EXAMPLE 2.TXT
This line is identical.
This is Example File 2.
Do you see the subtle difference?
*****

C:\Users\Tina>
```

File Compare

You can use this command to identify differences in text between two files. It's particularly useful for writers and programmers trying to find small changes between two versions of a file. Simply type **fc** and then the directory path and file name of the two files you want to compare.

You can also extend the command in several ways. Typing **/b** compares only binary output, **/c** disregards the case of text in the comparison, and **/l** only compares ASCII text.

So, for example, you could use the following:

- fc /l "C:\Program Files (x86)\example1.doc" "C:\Program Files (x86)\example2.doc"

The above command compares ASCII text in two Word documents.

5. *Ipconfig*

COMMAND PROMPT

```
C:\Windows\system32\cmd.exe                                    —    □    ×

Windows IP Configuration

Ethernet adapter Ethernet:

   Connection-specific DNS Suffix  . : telus
   IPv6 Address. . . . . . . . . . . :
   Temporary IPv6 Address. . . . . . :
   Link-local IPv6 Address . . . . . :
   IPv4 Address. . . . . . . . . . . :
   Subnet Mask . . . . . . . . . . . :
   Default Gateway . . . . . . . . . :

Wireless LAN adapter Local Area Connection* 1:

   Media State . . . . . . . . . . . : Media disconnected
   Connection-specific DNS Suffix  . :
```

Ipconfig

This command relays the IP address that your computer is currently using. However, if you're behind a router (like most computers today), you'll instead receive the local network address of the router.

Still, ipconfig is useful because of its extensions. **ipconfig /release** followed by **ipconfig /renew** can force your Windows PC into asking for a new IP address, which is useful if your computer claims one isn't available. You can also use **ipconfig /flushdns** to refresh your DNS address. These commands are great if the Windows network troubleshooter chokes, which does happen on occasion.

6. *Netstat*

Netstat

Entering the command **netstat -an** will provide you with a list of currently open ports and related IP addresses. This command will also tell you what state the port is in; listening, established, or closed.

This is a great command for when you're trying to troubleshoot devices connected to your PC or when you fear a Trojan infected your system and you're trying to locate a malicious connection.

7. Ping

```
C:\Windows\system32\cmd.exe

C:\Users\Tina>ping

Usage: ping [-t] [-a] [-n count] [-l size] [-f] [-i TTL] [-v TOS]
            [-r count] [-s count] [[-j host-list] | [-k host-list]]
            [-w timeout] [-R] [-S srcaddr] [-c compartment] [-p]
            [-4] [-6] target_name

Options:
    -t              Ping the specified host until stopped.
                    To see statistics and continue - type Control-Break;
                    To stop - type Control-C.
    -a              Resolve addresses to hostnames.
    -n count        Number of echo requests to send.
    -l size         Send buffer size.
    -f              Set Don't Fragment flag in packet (IPv4-only).
    -i TTL          Time To Live.
    -v TOS          Type Of Service (IPv4-only. This setting has been deprecated
                    and has no effect on the type of service field in the IP
```

Ping

Sometimes, you need to know whether or not packets are making it to a specific networked device. That's where ping comes in handy.

Typing **ping** followed by an IP address or web domain will send a series of test packets to the specified address. If they arrive and are returned, you know the device is capable of communicating with your PC; if it fails, you know that there's something blocking communication between the device and your computer. This can help you decide if the root of the issue is an improper configuration or a failure of network hardware.

8. PathPing

```
C:\Users\Tina>pathping

Usage: pathping [-g host-list] [-h maximum_hops] [-i address] [-n]
                [-p period] [-q num_queries] [-w timeout]
                [-4] [-6] target_name

Options:
    -g host-list     Loose source route along host-list.
    -h maximum_hops  Maximum number of hops to search for target.
    -i address       Use the specified source address.
    -n               Do not resolve addresses to hostnames.
    -p period        Wait period milliseconds between pings.
    -q num_queries   Number of queries per hop.
    -w timeout       Wait timeout milliseconds for each reply.
    -4               Force using IPv4.
    -6               Force using IPv6.

C:\Users\Tina>
```

PathPing

This is a more advanced version of ping that's useful if there are multiple routers between your PC and the device you're testing. Like ping, you use this command by typing **pathping** followed by the IP address, but unlike ping, pathping also relays some information about the route the test packets take.

9. Tracert

```
C:\Users\Tina>tracert google.com

Tracing route to google.com [2607:f8b0:400a:800::200e]
over a maximum of 30 hops:

  1   121 ms     5 ms   127 ms  node-1w7jr9qr7y81tri3xgl4k7z3k.ipv6.telus.net [20
01:569:7a3e:2500:9e1e:95ff:feae:2170]
  2    54 ms   132 ms   132 ms  node-1w7jr9n23go7xxm8nxwy3e630.ipv6.telus.net [20
01:568:ff00:f::14c]
  3   195 ms   133 ms   130 ms  node-1w7jr9fenjgbk2vrqtjijbdp6.ipv6.telus.net [20
01:568:1::51a]
  4    58 ms   133 ms   131 ms  2001:4860:1:1::d16
  5    60 ms   132 ms   138 ms  2001:4860:0:1041::1
  6    67 ms   131 ms   139 ms  2001:4860:0:1::1e6f
  7    64 ms   133 ms   130 ms  sea15s07-in-x0e.1e100.net [2607:f8b0:400a:800::20
0e]

Trace complete.
```

Tracert

The **tracert** command is similar to pathping. Once again, type **tracert** followed by the IP address or domain you'd like to trace. You'll receive information about each step in the route between your PC and the target. Unlike pathping, however, tracert also tracks how much time (in milliseconds) each hop between servers or devices takes.

10. Powercfg

```
C:\Windows\system32\cmd.exe
C:\Users\Tina>powercfg /a
The following sleep states are available on this system:
    Standby (S3)
    Hibernate
    Hybrid Sleep
    Fast Startup

The following sleep states are not available on this system:
    Standby (S1)
        The system firmware does not support this standby state.

    Standby (S2)
        The system firmware does not support this standby state.

    Standby (S0 Low Power Idle)
        The system firmware does not support this standby state.
```

Powercfg

Powercfg is a very powerful command for managing and tracking how your computer uses energy. You can use the command **powercfg hibernate on** and **powercfg hibernate off** to manage hibernation, and you can also use the command **powercfg /a** to view the power-saving states currently available on your PC.

Another useful command is **powercfg /devicequery s1_supported**, which displays a list of devices on your computer that support connected standby. When enabled, you can use these devices to bring your computer out of standby, even remotely.

You can enable this by selecting the device in **Device Manager**, opening its properties, going to the **Power Management** tab, and then checking the **Allow this device to wake the computer box**.

Powercfg /lastwake will show you what device last woke your PC from a sleep state. You can use this command to troubleshoot your PC if it seems to wake from sleep at random.

```
C:\Windows\system32>powercfg
Invalid Parameters -- try "/?" for help

C:\Windows\system32>powercfg /energy
Enabling tracing for 60 seconds...
Observing system behavior...
Analyzing trace data...
Analysis complete.

Energy efficiency problems were found.

12 Errors
29 Warnings
105 Informational

See C:\Windows\system32\energy-report.html for more details.

C:\Windows\system32>
```

Powercfg

You can use the **powercfg /energy** command to build a detailed power consumption report for your PC. The report saves to the directory indicated after the command finishes.

This report will let you know of any system faults that might increase power consumption, like devices blocking certain sleep modes, or poorly configured to respond to your power management settings.

Windows 8 added **powercfg /batteryreport**, which provides a detailed analysis of battery use, if applicable. Normally output to your Windows user directory, the report provides details about the time and length of charge and discharge cycles, lifetime average battery life, and estimated battery capacity.

11. Shutdown

```
Administrator: Command Prompt                                      —    □    ×

C:\Windows\system32>shutdown
Usage: shutdown [/i | /l | /s | /sg | /r | /g | /a | /p | /h | /e | /o] [/hybrid]
  [/soft] [/fw] [/f]
    [/m \\computer][/t xxx][/d [p|u:]xx:yy [/c "comment"]]

    No args     Display help. This is the same as typing /?.
    /?          Display help. This is the same as not typing any options.
    /i          Display the graphical user interface (GUI).
                This must be the first option.
    /l          Log off. This cannot be used with /m or /d options.
    /s          Shutdown the computer.
    /sg         Shutdown the computer. On the next boot,
                restart any registered applications.
    /r          Full shutdown and restart the computer.
    /g          Full shutdown and restart the computer. After the system is
                rebooted, restart any registered applications.
    /a          Abort a system shutdown.
                This can only be used during the time-out period.
```

Shutdown

Windows 8 introduced the shutdown command that, you guessed it, shuts down your computer.

This is, of course, redundant with the already easily accessed shutdown button, but what's not redundant is the **shutdown /r /o** command, which restarts your PC and launches the Advanced Start Options menu, which is where you can access Safe Mode and Windows recovery utilities. This is useful if you want to restart your computer for troubleshooting purposes.

12. Systeminfo

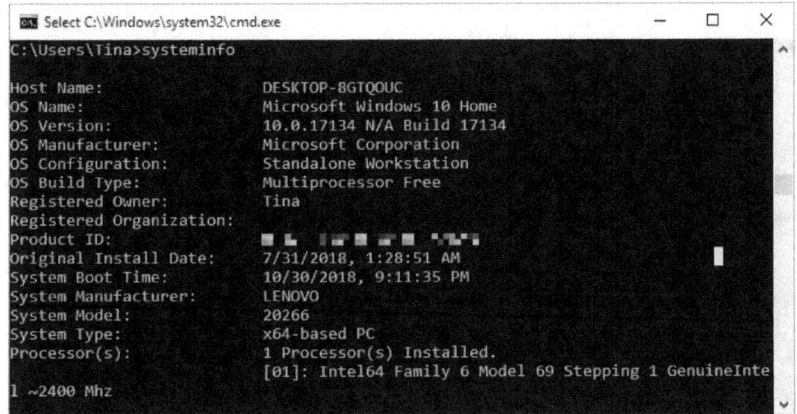

Systeminfo

This command will give you a detailed configuration overview of your computer. The list covers your operating system and hardware. For example, you can look up the original Windows installation date, the last boot time, your BIOS version, total and available memory, installed hotfixes, network card configurations, and more.

Use **systeminfo /s** followed by the hostname of a computer on your local network, to remotely grab the information for that system. This may require additional syntax elements for the domain, user name, and password, like this:

- **systeminfo /s [host_name] /u [domain]\[user_name] /p [user_password]**

13. System File Checker

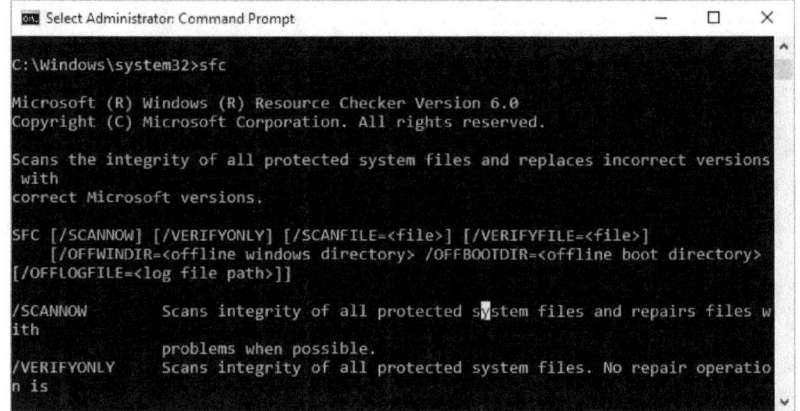

System File Checker

System File Checker is an automatic scan and repair tool that focuses on Windows system files.

You will need to run the command prompt with administrator privileges and enter the command **sfc /scannow**. If SFC finds any corrupt or missing files, it will automatically replace them using cached copies kept by Windows for this purpose alone. The command can require a half-hour to run on older notebooks.

14. Tasklist

```
Administrator: Command Prompt                                    —    □    ×

C:\Windows\system32>tasklist

Image Name                     PID Session Name        Session#    Mem Usage
========================= ======== ================ =========== ============
System Idle Process              0 Services                   0          8 K
System                           4 Services                   0     11,220 K
Registry                        96 Services                   0     15,380 K
smss.exe                       360 Services                   0        140 K
csrss.exe                      512 Services                   0      1,344 K
wininit.exe                    616 Services                   0         20 K
csrss.exe                      624 Console                    1      2,356 K
winlogon.exe                   724 Console                    1      3,884 K
services.exe                   768 Services                   0      4,820 K
lsass.exe                      808 Services                   0     11,892 K
svchost.exe                    920 Services                   0        220 K
fontdrvhost.exe                940 Services                   0      1,264 K
fontdrvhost.exe                944 Console                    1      2,040 K
svchost.exe                    968 Services                   0     19,656 K
```

Tasklist

You can use the tasklist command to provide a current list of all tasks running on your PC. Though somewhat redundant with Task Manager, the command may sometimes find tasks hidden from view in that utility.

There's also a wide range of modifiers. **Tasklist -svc** shows services related to each task, use **tasklist -v** to obtain more detail on each task, and **tasklist -m** will locate DLL files associated with active tasks. These commands are useful for advanced troubleshooting.

Our reader Eric noted that you can "get the name of the executable associated with the particular process ID you're interested in." The command for that operation is **tasklist | find [process id]**.

15. Taskkill

```
Administrator: Command Prompt                                    —   □   ×
i_view64.exe              19668 Console           1      37,804 K
cmd.exe                    1272 Console           1       2,948 K
conhost.exe               20612 Console           1      10,284 K
chrome.exe                19756 Console           1     109,324 K
cmd.exe                   15192 Console           1       3,208 K
conhost.exe               20132 Console           1      15,680 K
SearchProtocolHost.exe     1988 Services          0      10,532 K
SearchFilterHost.exe      10564 Services          0       7,524 K
tasklist.exe              12328 Console           1       7,300 K
WmiPrvSE.exe              11648 Services          0       8,572 K

C:\Windows\system32>taskkill
ERROR: Invalid syntax. Neither /FI nor /PID nor /IM were specified.
Type "TASKKILL /?" for usage.

C:\Windows\system32>taskkill -pid 19668
SUCCESS: Sent termination signal to the process with PID 19668.

C:\Windows\system32>
```

Taskkill

Tasks that appear in the **tasklist** command will have an executable and process ID (a four- or five-digit number) associated with them. You can force stop a program using **taskkill -im** followed by the executable's name, or **taskkill -pid** followed by the process ID. Again, this is a bit redundant with Task Manager, but you can use it to kill otherwise unresponsive or hidden programs.

16. Chkdsk

Chkdsk

Windows automatically marks your drive for a diagnostic chkdsk scan when symptoms indicate that a local drive has bad sectors, lost clusters, or other logical or physical errors.

If you suspect your hard drive is failing, you can manually initiate a scan. The most basic command is **chkdsk c:**, which will immediately scan the C: drive, without a need to restart the computer. If you add parameters like **/f, /r, /x, or /b**, such as in **chkdsk /f /r /x /b c:**, **chkdsk** will also fix errors, recover data, dismount the drive, or clear the list of bad sectors, respectively. These actions require a reboot, as they can only run with Windows powered down.

17. Schtasks

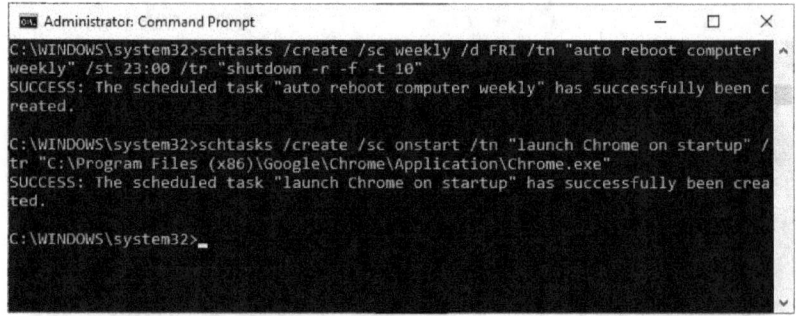

Schtasks

Schtasks is your command prompt access to the Task Scheduler, one of many underrated Windows administrative tools. While you can use the GUI to manage your scheduled tasks, the command prompt lets you copy&paste complex commands to set up multiple similar tasks without having to click through various options. Ultimately, it's much easier to use, once you've committed key parameters to memory.

For example, you could schedule your computer to reboot at 11PM every Friday:

- schtasks /create /sc weekly /d FRI /tn "auto reboot computer weekly" /st 23:00 /tr "shutdown -r -f -t 10"

To complement your weekly reboot, you could schedule tasks to launch specific programs on startup:

- schtasks /create /sc onstart /tn "launch Chrome on startup" /tr "C:\Program Files (x86)\Google\Chrome\Application\Chrome.exe"

To duplicate the above command for different programs, just copy, paste, and modify it as needed.

18. Format

```
Administrator: Command Prompt
C:\WINDOWS\system32>format D: /Q /FS:exFAT /A:2048 /V:label
Insert new disk for drive D:
and press ENTER when ready...
The type of the file system is EXFAT.
QuickFormatting 15.2 GB
Initializing the File Allocation Table (FAT)...
Creating file system structures.
Format complete.
     15.2 GB total disk space.
     15.2 GB are available.

     2,048 bytes in each allocation unit.
     7,975,701 allocation units available on disk.

          32 bits in each FAT entry.

Volume Serial Number is 7A5F-6DCE
```

Format

When you need to **format a drive,** you can either use the Windows File Explorer GUI or you can turn to the command prompt. You'll need Administrator rights to use this command. Be sure you specify the volume you want to format, followed by the desired parameters.

The command below will quick-format the D drive with the **exFAT file system**, with an allocation unit size of 2048 bytes, and rename the volume to "label" (without the quotes).

- format D: /Q /FS:exFAT /A:2048 /V:label

You can also use this command to dismount a volume (/X) or, if it's formatted with NTFS, make file compression the default setting (/R). If you're stuck, use format /? to summon help.

19. Prompt

Prompt

Would you like to customize your command prompt to include instructions or certain information? With the prompt command, you can!

Try this one:

- **prompt Your wish is my command:**

You can add the current time, date, drive and path, Windows version number, and so much more.

- **prompt $t on $d at $p using $v:**

Type "prompt" to reset your command prompt to default settings or just restart the command prompt. Unfortunately, these settings aren't permanent.

20. cls (Clears the screen)

Cluttered up your command prompt window trying out all the commands above? There's one last command you need to know to clean it all up again.

- cls

CHAPTER THREE

COMMAND PROMPT(CMD) COMMANDS

List of Command Prompt Commands

1. Append
   The append command can be used by programs to open files in another directory as if they were located in the current directory. The append command is available in MS-DOS as well as in all 32-bit versions of Windows. The append command is not available in 64-bit versions of Windows.
2. Arp
   The arp command is used to display or change entries in the ARP cache. The arp command is available in all versions of Windows.
3. Assoc
   The assoc command is used to display or change the file type associated with a particular file extension. The assoc command is available in Windows 10, Windows 8, Windows 7, Windows Vista, and Windows XP.
4. At
   The at command is used to schedule commands and other programs to run at a specific date and time. The at command

is available in Windows 7, Windows Vista, and Windows XP. Beginning in Windows 8, command line task scheduling should instead be completed with the schtasks command.https://www.lifewire.com/at-command-2618090

5. Atmadm

   The atmadm command is used to display information related to asynchronous transfer mode (ATM) connections on the system. The atmadm command is available in Windows XP. Support for ATM was removed beginning in Windows Vista, making the atmadm command unnecessary.

6. Attrib

   The attrib command is used to change the attributes of a single file or a directory. The attrib command is available in all versions of Windows, as well as in MS-DOS.

7. Auditpol

   The auditpol command is used to display or change audit policies. The auditpol command is available in Windows 10, Windows 8, Windows 7, and Windows Vista.

8. Bcdboot

   The bcdboot command is used to copy boot files to the system partition and to create a new system BCD store. The bcdboot command is available in Windows 10, Windows 8, and Windows 7.

9. Bcdedit

   The bcdedit command is used to view or make changes to Boot Configuration Data. The bcdedit command is available in Windows 10, Windows 8, Windows 7, and Windows Vista. The bcdedit command replaced the bootcfg command beginning in Windows Vista.

10. Bdehdcfg

    The bdehdcfg command is used to prepare a hard drive for BitLocker Drive Encryption. The bdehdcfg command is available in Windows 10, Windows 8, and Windows 7.

11. Bitsadmin

    The bitsadmin command is used to create, manage, and monitor download and upload jobs. The bitsadmin command is available in Windows 8, Windows 7, and Windows Vista. While the bitsadmin command is available in both Windows 8 and Windows 7, it is being phased out. The BITS PowerShell cmdlets should be used instead.

12. Bootcfg

    The bootcfg command is used to build, modify, or view the contents of the boot.ini file, a hidden file that is used to identify in what folder, on which partition, and on which hard drive Windows is located. The bootcfg command is available in Windows 10, Windows 8, Windows 7, Windows Vista, and Windows XP. The bootcfg command was replaced by the bcdedit command beginning in Windows Vista. Bootcfg is still available in Windows 10, 8, 7, and Vista, but it serves no real value since boot.ini is not used in these operating systems.

13. Bootsect

    The bootsect command is used to configure the master boot code to one compatible with BOOTMGR (Vista and later) or NTLDR (XP and earlier). The bootsect command is available in Windows 10 and Windows 8. The bootsect command is also available in Windows 7 and Windows Vista but only from the Command Prompt available in System Recovery Options.

14. Break

    The break command sets or clears extended CTRL+C checking on DOS systems. The break command is available in all versions of Windows, as well as in MS-DOS. The break command is available in Windows XP and later versions of Windows to provide compatibility with MS-DOS files but it has no effect in Windows itself.

15. Cacls

    The cacls command is used to display or change access control lists of files. The cacls command is available in Windows 10, Windows 8, Windows 7, Windows Vista, and Windows XP. The cacls command is being phased out in favor of the icacls command, which should be used instead in all versions of

Windows after Windows XP.

16. Call

    The call command is used to run a script or batch program from within another script or batch program. The call command is available in all versions of Windows, as well as in MS-DOS. The call command has no effect outside of a script or batch file. In other words, running the call command at the Command Prompt or MS-DOS prompt will do nothing.

17. Cd

    The cd command is the shorthand version of the chdir command. The cd command is available in all versions of Windows, as well as in MS-DOS.

18. Certreq

    The certreq command is used to perform various certification authority (CA) certificate functions. The certreq command is available in Windows 10, Windows 8, Windows 7, and Windows Vista.

19. Certutil

    The certutil command is used to dump and display certification authority (CA) configuration information in addition to other CA functions. The certutil command is available in Windows 10, Windows 8, Windows 7, and Windows Vista.

20. Change

    The change command changes various terminal server settings like install modes, COM port mappings, and logons. The change command is available in Windows 10, Windows 8, Windows 7, and Windows Vista.

21. Chcp

    The chcp command displays or configures the active code page number. The chcp command is available in all versions of Windows, as well as in MS-DOS.

22. Chdir

    The chdir command is used to display the drive letter and folder that you are currently in. Chdir can also be used to change the drive and/or directory that you want to work in. The chdir command is available in all versions of Windows, as well as in MS-DOS.

23. Checknetisolation

    The checknetisolation command is used to test apps that require network capabilities. The checknetisolation command is available in Windows 10 and Windows 8.

24. Chglogon

    The chglogon command enables, disables, or drains terminal server session logins. The chglogon command is available in Windows 10, Windows 8, Windows 7, and Windows Vista. Executing the chglogon command is the same as executing change logon.

25. Chgport

    The chgport command can be used to display or change COM port mappings for DOS compatibility. The chgport command is available in Windows 10, Windows 8, Windows 7, and Windows Vista. Executing the chgport command is the same as executing change port.

26. Chgusr

    The chgusr command is used to change the install mode for the terminal server. The chgusr command is available in Windows 10, Windows 8, Windows 7, and Windows Vista. Executing the chgusr command is the same as executing change user.

27. Chkdsk

    The chkdsk command, often referred to as check disk, is used to identify and correct certain hard drive errors. The chkdsk command is available in all versions of Windows, as well as in MS-DOS.

28. Chkntfs

    The chkntfs command is used to configure or display the checking of the disk drive during the Windows boot process. The chkntfs command is available in Windows 10, Windows 8, Windows 7, Windows Vista, and Windows XP.

29. Choice

    The choice command is used within a script or batch program to provide a list of choices and return the value of that choice to the program. The choice command is available in MS-DOS and all versions of Windows except Windows XP. Use the set command with the /p switch in place of the choice command in batch files and scripts that you plan to use in Windows XP.

30. Cipher

The cipher command shows or changes the encryption status of files and folders on NTFS partitions. The cipher command is available in Windows 10, Windows 8, Windows 7, Windows Vista, and Windows XP.

31. Clip

The clip command is used to redirect the output from any command to the clipboard in Windows. The clip command is available in Windows 10, Windows 8, Windows 7, and Windows Vista.

32. Cls

The cls command clears the screen of all previously entered commands and other text. The cls command is available in all versions of Windows, as well as in MS-DOS.

33. Cmd

The cmd command starts a new instance of the cmd.exe command interpreter. The cmd command is available in Windows 10, Windows 8, Windows 7, Windows Vista, and Windows XP.

34. Cmdkey

The cmdkey command is used to show, create, and remove stored user names and passwords. The cmdkey command is available in Windows 10, Windows 8, Windows 7, and Windows Vista.

35. Cmstp

The cmstp command installs or uninstalls a Connection Manager service profile. The cmstp command is available in Windows 10, Windows 8, Windows 7, Windows Vista, and Windows XP.

36. Color

    The color command is used to change the colors of the text and background within the Command Prompt window. The color command is available in Windows 10, Windows 8, Windows 7, Windows Vista, and Windows XP.

37. Command

    The command command starts a new instance of the command.com command interpreter. The command command is available in MS-DOS as well as in all 32-bit versions of Windows. The command command is not available in 64-bit versions of Windows.

38. Comp

    The comp command is used to compare the contents of two files or sets of files. The comp command is available in Windows 10, Windows 8, Windows 7, Windows Vista, and Windows XP.

39. Compact

    The compact command is used to show or change the compression state of files and directories on NTFS partitions. The compact command is available in Windows 10, Windows 8, Windows 7, Windows Vista, and Windows XP.

40. Convert

    The convert command is used to convert FAT or FAT32 formatted volumes to the NTFS format. The convert command is available in Windows 10, Windows 8, Windows 7, Windows Vista, and Windows XP.

41. Copy

    The copy command does simply that — it copies one or more files from one location to another. The copy command is available in all versions of Windows, as well as in MS-DOS. The xcopy command is considered to be a more "powerful" version of the copy command.

42. Cscript

    The cscript command is used to execute scripts via Microsoft Script Host. The cscript command is available in all versions of Windows. The cscript command is most popularly used to manage printers from the command line using scripts like prncnfg.vbs, prndrvr.vbs, prnmngr.vbs, and others.

43. Ctty

The ctty command is used to change the default input and output devices for the system. The ctty command is available in Windows 98 and 95 as well as in MS-DOS. The functions provided by the ctty command were no longer necessary beginning in Windows XP because the command.com interpreter (MS-DOS) is no longer the default command line interpreter.

44. Date

The date command is used to show or change the current date. The date command is available in all versions of Windows, as well as in MS-DOS.

45. Dblspace

The dblspace command is used to create or configure DoubleSpace compressed drives. The dblspace command is available in Windows 98 and 95, as well as in MS-DOS. DriveSpace, executed using the drvspace command, is an updated version of DoubleSpace. Windows began handling compression beginning in Windows XP.

46. Debug

The debug command starts Debug, a command line application used to test and edit programs. The debug command is available in MS-DOS as well as in all 32-bit versions of Windows. The debug command is not available in 64-bit versions of Windows.

47. Defrag

The defrag command is used to defragment a drive you specify. The defrag command is the command line version of Microsoft's Disk Defragmenter. The defrag command is available in all versions of Windows, as well as in MS-DOS.

48. Del

The del command is used to delete one or more files. The del command is available in all versions of Windows, as well as in MS-DOS. The del command is the same as the erase command.

49. Deltree

    The deltree command is used to delete a directory and all the files and subdirectories within it. The deltree command is available in Windows 98 and 95, as well as in MS-DOS. Beginning in Windows XP, a folder and its files and subfolders can be removed using the /s function of the rmdir command. Deltree was no longer needed with this new rmdir ability so the command was removed.

50. Diantz

    The diantz command is used to losslessly compress one or more files. The diantz command is sometimes called Cabinet Maker. The diantz command is available in Windows 7, Windows Vista, and Windows XP. The diantz command is the same as the makecab command.

51. Dir

    The dir command is used to display a list of files and folders contained inside the folder that you are currently working in. The dir command also displays other important information like the hard drive's serial number, the total number of files listed, their combined size, the total amount of free space left on the drive, and more. The dir command is available in all versions of Windows, as well as in MS-DOS.

52. Diskcomp

    The diskcomp command is used to compare the contents of two floppy disks. The diskcomp command is available in all versions of Windows, as well as in MS-DOS, with the exclusion of Windows 10.

53. Diskcopy

    The diskcopy command is used to copy the entire contents of one floppy disk to another. The diskcopy command is available in all versions of Windows, as well as in MS-DOS, with the exclusion of Windows 10.

54. Diskpart

    The diskpart command is used to create, manage, and delete hard drive partitions. The diskpart command is available in

Windows 8, Windows 7, Windows Vista, and Windows XP. The diskpart command replaced the fdisk command beginning in Windows XP.

55. Diskperf

The diskperf command is used to manage disk performance counters remotely. The diskperf command is available in Windows 10, Windows 8, Windows 7, Windows Vista, and Windows XP.

56. Diskraid

The diskraid command starts the DiskRAID tool which is used to manage and configure RAID arrays. The diskraid command is available in Windows 10, Windows 8, Windows 7, and Windows Vista.

57. Dism

The dism command starts the Deployment Image Servicing and Management tool (DISM). The DISM tool is used to manage features in Windows images. The dism command is available in Windows 10, Windows 8, and Windows 7.

58. Dispdiag

The dispdiag command is used to output a log of information about the display system. The dispdiag command is available in Windows 10, Windows 8, Windows 7, and Windows Vista.

59. Djoin

The djoin command is used to create a new computer account in a domain. The djoin command is available in Windows 10, Windows 8, Windows 7, and Windows Vista.

60. Doskey

The doskey command is used to edit command lines, create macros, and recall previously entered commands. The doskey command is available in all versions of Windows, as well as in MS-DOS.

61. Dosshell

The dosshell command starts DOS Shell, a graphical file management tool for MS-DOS. The dosshell command is available in Windows 95 (in MS-DOS mode) and also in MS-

DOS version 6.0 and later MS-DOS versions that were upgraded from previous versions that contained the dosshell command. A graphical file manager, Windows Explorer, became an integrated part of the operating system beginning in Windows 95.

62. Dosx

The dosx command is used to start DOS Protected Mode Interface (DPMI), a special mode designed to give MS-DOS applications access to more than the normally allowed 640 KB. The dosx command is available in Windows 10, Windows 8, Windows 7, Windows Vista, and Windows XP. The dosx command is not available in 64-bit versions of Windows. The dosx command and DPMI is only available in Windows to support older MS-DOS programs.

63. Driverquery

The driverquery command is used to show a list of all installed drivers. The driverquery command is available in Windows 10, Windows 8, Windows 7, Windows Vista, and Windows XP.

64. Drvspace

The drvspace command is used to create or configure DriveSpace compressed drives. The drvspace command is available in Windows 98 and 95, as well as in MS-DOS. DriveSpace is an updated version of DoubleSpace, executed using the dblspace command. Windows began handling compression beginning in Windows XP.

65. Echo

The echo command is used to show messages, most commonly from within script or batch files. The echo command can also be used to turn the echoing feature on or off. The echo command is available in all versions of Windows, as well as in MS-DOS.

66. Edit

The edit command starts the MS-DOS Editor tool which is used to create and modify text files. The edit command is available in MS-DOS as well as in all 32-bit versions of Windows. The edit command is not available in 64-bit versions of Windows.

67. Edlin

    The edlin command starts the Edlin tool which is used to create and modify text files from the command line. The edlin command is available in all 32-bit versions of Windows but is not available in 64-bit versions of Windows. In MS-DOS, the edlin command is only available up to MS-DOS 5.0, so unless your later version of MS-DOS was upgraded from 5.0 or prior, you won't see the edlin command.

68. Emm386

    The emm386 command is used to give MS-DOS access to more than 640 KB of memory (RAM). The emm386 command is available in Windows 98 and 95, as well as in MS-DOS. Windows itself has access to extended and expanded memory beginning in Windows 95.

69. Endlocal

    The endlocal command is used to end the localization of environment changes inside a batch or script file. The endlocal command is available in Windows 10, Windows 8, Windows 7, Windows Vista, and Windows XP.

70. Erase

    The erase command is used to delete one or more files. The erase command is available in all versions of Windows, as well as in MS-DOS. The erase command is the same as the del command.

71. Esentutl

    The esentutl command is used to manage Extensible Storage Engine databases. The esentutl command is available in Windows 10, Windows 8, Windows 7, Windows Vista, and Windows XP.

72. Eventcreate

    The eventcreate command is used to create a custom event in an event log. The eventcreate command is available in Windows 10, Windows 8, Windows 7, Windows Vista, and Windows XP.

73. Eventtriggers

    The eventtriggers command is used to configure and display

event triggers. The eventtriggers command is available in Windows XP. Beginning in Windows Vista, event triggers are created using the Attach Task To This Event feature in Event Viewer, making the eventtriggers command unnecessary.

74. Exe2bin

    The exe2bin command is used to convert a file of the EXE file type (executable file) to a binary file. The exe2bin command is available in 32-bit versions of Windows 10, Windows 8, Windows 7, Windows Vista, and Windows XP. The exe2bin command is not available in any 64-bit version of Windows.

75. Exit

    The exit command is used to end the cmd.exe (Windows) or command.com (MS-DOS) session that you're currently working in. The exit command is available in all versions of Windows, as well as in MS-DOS.

76. Expand The expand command is used to extract the files and folders contained in Microsoft Cabinet (CAB) files. The expand command is available in MS-DOS as well as in all versions of Windows. The expand command is not available in the 64-bit version of Windows XP.

77. Extrac32

    The extrac32 command is used to extract the files and folders contained in Microsoft Cabinet (CAB) files. The extrac32 command is available in all versions of Windows. The extrac32 command is actually a CAB extraction program for use by Internet Explorer but can be used to extract any Microsoft Cabinet file. Use the expand command instead of the extrac32 command if possible.

78. Extract

    The extract command is used to extract the files and folders contained in Microsoft Cabinet (CAB) files. The extract command is available in Windows 98 and 95. The extract command was replaced by the expand command beginning in Windows XP.

79. Fasthelp

    The fasthelp command provides more detailed information on any of the other MS-DOS commands. The fasthelp command is only available in MS-DOS. The help command replaced the fasthelp command beginning in Windows 95.

80. Fastopen

    The fastopen command is used to add a program's hard drive location to a special list stored in memory, potentially improving the program's launch time by removing the need for MS-DOS to locate the application on the drive. The fastopen command is available in MS-DOS as well as in all 32-bit versions of Windows. The fastopen command is not available in 64-bit versions of Windows. Fastopen is only available in Windows 10, Windows 8, 7, Vista, and XP to support older MS-DOS files.

81. Fc

    The fc command is used to compare two individual or sets of files and then show the differences between them. The fc command is available in all versions of Windows, as well as in MS-DOS.

82. Fdisk

    The fdisk command is used to create, manage, and delete hard drive partitions. The fdisk command is available in Windows 98 and 95, as well as in MS-DOS. The fdisk command was replaced by the diskpart command beginning in Windows XP. Partition management is also available from Disk Management in Windows 10, 8, 7, Vista, and XP.

83. Find

    The find command is used to search for a specified text string in one or more files. The find command is available in all versions of Windows, as well as in MS-DOS.

84. Findstr

    The findstr command is used to find text string patterns in one or more files. The findstr command is available in Windows 10, Windows 8, Windows 7, Windows Vista, and Windows XP.

85. Finger

    The finger command is used to return information about one or more users on a remote computer that's running the Finger service. The finger command is available in Windows 10, Windows 8, Windows 7, Windows Vista, and Windows XP.

86. Fltmc

    The fltmc command is used to load, unload, list, and otherwise manage Filter drivers. The fltmc command is available in Windows 10, Windows 8, Windows 7, Windows Vista, and Windows XP.

87. Fondue

    The fondue command, short for Features on Demand User Experience Tool, is used to install any of the several optional Windows features from the command line. The fondue command is available in Windows 8. Optional Windows features can also be installed from the Programs and Features applet in Control Panel.

88. For

    The for command is used to run a specified command for each file in a set of files. The for command is most often used within a batch or script file. The for command is available in all versions of Windows, as well as in MS-DOS.

89. Forcedos

    The forcedos command is used to start the specified program in the MS-DOS subsystem. The forcedos command is only available in 32-bit versions of Windows XP. The forcedos command is only used for MS-DOS programs that are not recognized as such by Windows XP.

90. Forfiles

    The forfiles command selects one or more files to execute a specified command on. The forfiles command is most often used within a batch or script file. The forfiles command is available in Windows 10, Windows 8, Windows 7, and Windows Vista.

91. Format

    The format command is used to format a drive in the file system that you specify. The format command is available in all versions of Windows, as well as in MS-DOS. Drive formatting is also available from Disk Management in Windows 10, 8, 7, Vista, and XP.

92. Fsutil

The fsutil command is used to perform various FAT and NTFS file system tasks like managing reparse points and sparse files, dismounting a volume, and extending a volume. The fsutil command is available in Windows 10, Windows 8, Windows 7, Windows Vista, and Windows XP.

93. Ftp

The ftp command can be used to transfer files to and from another computer. The remote computer must be operating as an FTP server. The ftp command is available in all versions of Windows.

94. Ftype

The ftype command is used to define a default program to open a specified file type. The ftype command is available in Windows 10, Windows 8, Windows 7, Windows Vista, and Windows XP.

95. Getmac

The getmac command is used to display the media access control (MAC) address of all the network controllers on a system. The getmac command is available in Windows 10, Windows 8, Windows 7, Windows Vista, and Windows XP.

96. Goto

The goto command is used in a batch or script file to direct the command process to a labeled line in the script. The goto command is available in all versions of Windows, as well as in MS-DOS.

97. Gpresult

The gpresult command is used to display Group Policy settings. The gpresult command is available in Windows 10, Windows 8, Windows 7, Windows Vista, and Windows XP.

98. Gpupdate

The gpupdate command is used to update Group Policy settings.

The gpupdate command is available in Windows 10, Windows 8, Windows 7, Windows Vista, and Windows XP.

99. Graftabl

The graftabl command is used to enable the ability of Windows to display an extended character set in graphics mode. The graftabl command is available in all versions of Windows and in MS-DOS up to version 5.0. The graftabl command is not available in 64-bit versions of Windows.

100. Graphics

The graphics command is used to load a program that can print graphics. The graphics command is available in MS-DOS as well as in all 32-bit versions of Windows. The graphics command is not available in 64-bit versions of Windows.

101. Help

The help command provides more detailed information on any of the other Command Prompt or MS-DOS commands. The help command is available in all versions of Windows, as well as in MS-DOS.

102. Hostname

The hostname command displays the name of the current host. The hostname command is available in Windows 10, Windows 8, Windows 7, Windows Vista, and Windows XP.

103. Hwrcomp

The hwrcomp command is used to compile custom dictionaries for handwriting recognition. The hwrcomp command is available in Windows 8 and Windows 7.

104. Hwrreg

The hwrreg command is used to install a previously compiled custom dictionary for handwriting recognition. The hwrreg command is available in Windows 8 and Windows 7.

105. Icacls

The icacls command is used to display or change access control lists of files. The icacls command is available in Windows 10, Windows 8, Windows 7, and Windows Vista. The icacls command is an updated version of the cacls command.

106. If
     The if command is used to perform conditional functions in a batch file. The if command is available in all versions of Windows, as well as in MS-DOS.
107. Interlnk
     The interlnk command is used to connect two computers via a serial or parallel connection to share files and printers. The interlnk command is only available in MS-DOS. The ability to directly connect two computers is handled by the networking functions in all versions of Windows.
108. Intersvr
     The intersvr command is used to start the Interlnk server and to copy Interlnk files from one computer to another. The intersvr command is only available in MS-DOS. The ability to directly connect two computers is handled by the networking functions in all versions of Windows.
109. Ipconfig
     The ipconfig command is used to display detailed IP information for each network adapter utilizing TCP/IP. The ipconfig command can also be used to release and renew IP addresses on systems configured to receive them via a DHCP server. The ipconfig command is available in all versions of Windows.
110. Ipxroute
     The ipxroute command is used to display and change information about IPX routing tables. The ipxroute command is available in Windows XP. Microsoft removed their built-in NetWare client beginning in Windows Vista, removing the associated ipxroute command as well.
111. Irftp
     The irftp command is used to transmit files over an infrared link. The irftp command is available in Windows 8, Windows 7, and Windows Vista.
112. Iscsicli
     The iscsicli command starts the Microsoft iSCSI Initiator, used to manage iSCSI. The iscsicli command is available in Windows

10, Windows 8, Windows 7, and Windows Vista.
113. Kb16

The kb16 command is used to support MS-DOS files that need to configure a keyboard for a specific language. The kb16 command is available in Windows 10, Windows 8, Windows 7, Windows Vista, and Windows XP. The kb16 command is not available in 64-bit versions of Windows. The kb16 command replaced the keyb command beginning in Windows XP but only exists to support older MS-DOS files.

114. Keyb

The keyb command is used to configure a keyboard for a specific language. The keyb command is available in Windows 98 and 95, as well as in MS-DOS. See the kb16 command for an equivalent command in later versions of Windows. Keyboard language settings are handled by the Region and Language or Regional and Language Options (depending on the version of Windows) Control Panel applets in Windows beginning in Windows XP.

115. Klist

The klist command is used to list Kerberos service tickets. The klist command can also be used to purge Kerberos tickets. The klist command is available in Windows 10, Windows 8 and Windows 7.

116. Ksetup

The ksetup command is used to configure connections to a Kerberos server. The ksetup command is available in Windows 10, Windows 8 and Windows 7.

117. Ktmutil

The ktmutil command starts the Kernel Transaction Manager utility. The ktmutil command is available in Windows 10, Windows 8, Windows 7, and Windows Vista.

118. Label

The label command is used to manage the volume label of a disk. The label command is available in all versions of Windows, as well as in MS-DOS.

119. Lh

The lh command is the shorthand version of the loadhigh command. The lh command is available in Windows 98 and 95, as well as in MS-DOS.

120. Licensingdiag

The licensingdiag command is a tool used to generate a text-based log and other data files that contain product activation and other Windows licensing information. The licensingdiag command is available in Windows 10 and Windows 8.

121. Loadfix

The loadfix command is used to load the specified program in the first 64K of memory and then runs the program. The loadfix command is available in MS-DOS as well as in all 32-bit versions of Windows. The loadfix command is not available in 64-bit versions of Windows.

122. Loadhigh

The loadhigh command is used to load a program into high memory and is usually used from within the autoexec.bat file. The loadhigh command is available in Windows 98 and 95, as well as in MS-DOS. Memory usage is handled automatically beginning in Windows XP.

123. Lock

The lock command is used to lock a drive, enabling direct disk access for a program. The lock command is only available in Windows 98 and 95. Drive locking is no longer available as of Windows XP.

124. Lodctr

The lodctr command is used to update registry values related to performance counters. The lodctr command is available in all versions of Windows.

125. Logman

The logman command is used to create and manage Event Trace Session and Performance logs. The logman command also supports many functions of Performance Monitor. The logman command is available in Windows 10, Windows 8, Windows 7,

Windows Vista, and Windows XP.

126. Logoff

The logoff command is used to terminate a session. The logoff command is available in Windows 10, Windows 8, Windows 7, Windows Vista, and Windows XP.

127. Lpq

The lpq command displays the status of a print queue on a computer running Line Printer Daemon (LPD). The lpq command is available in all versions of Windows. The lpq command is not available by default in Windows 10, 8, 7, or Vista, but can be enabled by turning on the LPD Print Service and LPR Port Monitor features from Programs and Features in Control Panel.

128. Lpr

The lpr command is used to send a file to a computer running Line Printer Daemon (LPD). The lpr command is available in all versions of Windows. The lpr command is not available by default in Windows 10, 8, 7, or Vista, but can be enabled by turning on the LPD Print Service and LPR Port Monitor features from Programs and Features in Control Panel.

129. Makecab

The makecab command is used to losslessly compress one or more files. The makecab command is sometimes called Cabinet Maker. The makecab command is available in Windows 10, Windows 8, Windows 7, Windows Vista, and Windows XP. The makecab command is the same as the diantz command, a command that was removed after Windows 7.

130. Manage-bde

The manage-bde command is used to configure BitLocker Drive Encryption from the command line. The manage-bde command is available in Windows 10, Windows 8, and Windows 7. A script by the name of manage-bde.wsf exists in Windows Vista and can be used with the cscript command to perform BitLocker tasks from the command line in that operating system.

131. Md

    The md command is the shorthand version of the mkdir command. The md command is available in all versions of Windows, as well as in MS-DOS.

132. Mem

    The mem command shows information about used and free memory areas and programs that are currently loaded into memory in the MS-DOS subsystem. The mem command is available in MS-DOS as well as in all 32-bit versions of Windows. The mem command is not available in 64-bit versions of Windows.

133. Memmaker

    The memmaker command is used to start MemMaker, a memory optimization tool. The memaker command is available in Windows 98 and 95, as well as in MS-DOS. Memory usage is automatically optimized beginning in Windows XP.

134. Mkdir

    The mkdir command is used to create a new folder. The mkdir command is available in all versions of Windows, as well as in MS-DOS.

135. Mklink

    The mklink command is used to create a symbolic link. The mklink command is available in Windows 10, Windows 8, Windows 7, and Windows Vista.

136. Mode

    The mode command is used to configure system devices, most often COM and LPT ports. The mode command is available in all versions of Windows, as well as in MS-DOS.

137. Mofcomp

    The mofcomp command properly displays the data within a Managed Object Format (MOF) file. The mofcomp command is available in all versions of Windows.

138. More

    The more command is used to display the information contained in a text file. The more command can also be used to paginate the results of any other Command Prompt or MS-DOS command. The more command is available in all versions of Windows, as well as in MS-DOS.

139. Mount

The mount command is used to mount Network File System (NFS) network shares. The mount command is available in Windows 7 and Windows Vista. The mount command is not available by default in Windows Vista or Windows 7 but can be enabled by turning on the Services for NFS Windows feature from Programs and Features in Control Panel. The mount command is not available in Windows 10 or 8 because Service for UNIX (SFU) was discontinued.

140. Mountvol

The mountvol command is used to display, create, or remove volume mount points. The mountvol command is available in Windows 10, Windows 8, Windows 7, Windows Vista, and Windows XP.

141. Move

The move command is used to move one or files from one folder to another. The move command is also used to rename directories. The move command is available in all versions of Windows, as well as in MS-DOS.

142. Mrinfo

The mrinfo command is used to provide information about a router's interfaces and neighbors. The mrinfo command is available in Windows 10, Windows 8, Windows 7, Windows Vista, and Windows XP.

143. Msav

The msav command starts Microsoft Antivirus. The msav command is only available in MS-DOS. Microsoft Antivirus was designed for MS-DOS and Windows 3.x only. Microsoft provides an optional virus protection suite called Microsoft Security Essentials for Windows XP and later operating systems, and third party antivirus tools are available for all versions of Windows.

144. Msbackup

    The msbackup command starts Microsoft Backup, a tool used to back up and restore one or more files. The msbackup command is only available in MS-DOS. The msbackup command was replaced with Microsoft Backup beginning in Windows 95 and then Backup and Restore in later versions of Windows.

145. Mscdex

    The mscdex command is used to provide CD-ROM access to MS-DOS. The mscdex command is available in Windows 98 and 95, as well as in MS-DOS. Windows provides access to CD-ROM drives for the MS-DOS subsystem beginning in Windows XP, so the mscdex command is unnecessary in this and later operating systems.

146. Msd

    The msd command starts Microsoft Diagnostics, a system information tool. The msd command is only available in MS-DOS. The msd command was replaced with System Information beginning in Windows 95.

147. Msg

    The msg command is used to send a message to a user. The msg command is available in Windows 10, Windows 8, Windows 7, Windows Vista, and Windows XP.

148. Msiexec

    The msiexec command is used to start Windows Installer, a tool used to install and configure software. The msiexec command is available in Windows 10, Windows 8, Windows 7, Windows Vista, and Windows XP.

149. Muiunattend

    The muiunattend command starts the Multilanguage User Interface unattended setup process. The muiunattend command is available in Windows 10, Windows 8, Windows 7, and Windows Vista.

150. Nbtstat

    The nbtstat command is used to show TCP/IP information and other statistical information about a remote computer. The nbtstat command is available in all versions of Windows.

151. Net

The net command is used to display, configure, and correct a wide variety of network settings. The net command is available in all versions of Windows.

152. Net1

The net1 command is used to display, configure, and correct a wide variety of network settings. The net1 command is available in Windows 10, Windows 8, Windows 7, Windows Vista, and Windows XP. The net command should be used instead of the net1 command. The net1 command was made available in Windows NT and Windows 2000 as a temporary fix for a Y2K issue that the net command had, which was corrected before the release of Windows XP. The net1 command remains in later versions of Windows only for compatibility with older programs and scripts that utilized the command.

153. Netcfg

The netcfg command is used to install the Windows Preinstallation Environment (WinPE), a lightweight version of Windows used to deploy workstations. The netcfg command is available in Windows 10, Windows 8, Windows 7, and Windows Vista.

154. Netsh

The netsh command is used to start Network Shell, a command-line utility used to manage the network configuration of the local, or a remote, computer. The netsh command is available in Windows 10, Windows 8, Windows 7, Windows Vista, and Windows XP.

155. Netstat

The netstat command is most commonly used to display all open network connections and listening ports. The netstat command is available in all versions of Windows.

156. Nfsadmin

The nfsadmin command is used to manage Server for NFS or Client for NFS from the command line. The nfsadmin command is available in Windows 7 and Windows Vista. The nfsadmin command is not available by default in Windows Vista or Windows 7 but can be enabled by turning on the Services for NFS Windows feature from Programs and Features in Control Panel. The nfsadmin command is not available in Windows 10 or 8 because Service for UNIX (SFU) was discontinued.

157. Nlsfunc

The nlsfunc command is used to load information specific to a particular country or region. The nlsfunc command is available in MS-DOS as well as in all 32-bit versions of Windows. The nlsfunc command is not available in 64-bit versions of Windows. Nlsfunc is only available in Windows 10, 8, 7, Vista, and XP to support older MS-DOS files.

158. Nltest

The nltest command is used to test secure channels between Windows computers in a domain and between domain controllers that are trusting other domains. The nltest command is available in Windows 10, Windows 8, and Windows 7.

159. Nslookup

The nslookup is most commonly used to display the hostname of an entered IP address. The nslookup command queries your configured DNS server to discover the IP address. The nslookup command is available in Windows 10, Windows 8, Windows 7, Windows Vista, and Windows XP.

160. Ntbackup

The ntbackup command is used to perform various backup functions from the Command Prompt or from within a batch or script file. The ntbackup command is available in Windows XP. The ntbackup command was replaced with the wbadmin beginning in Windows Vista.

161. Ntsd

The ntsd command is used to perform certain command line debugging tasks. The ntsd command is available in Windows XP. The ntsd command was removed beginning in Windows Vista due to the addition of dump file support in Task Manager.

162. Ocsetup

    The ocsetup command starts the Windows Optional Component Setup tool, used to install additional Windows features. The ocsetup command is available in Windows 8, Windows 7, and Windows Vista. Beginning in Windows 8, Microsoft is depreciating the ocsetup command in favor of the dism command.

163. Openfiles

    The openfiles command is used to display and disconnect open files and folders on a system. The openfiles command is available in Windows 10, Windows 8, Windows 7, Windows Vista, and Windows XP.

164. Path

    The path command is used to display or set a specific path available to executable files. The path command is available in all versions of Windows, as well as in MS-DOS.

165. Pathping

    The pathping command functions much like the tracert command but will also report information about network latency and loss at each hop. The pathping command is available in Windows 10, Windows 8, Windows 7, Windows Vista, and Windows XP.

166. Pause

    The pause command is used within a batch or script file to pause the processing of the file. When the pause command is used, a "Press any key to continue..." message displays in the command window. The pause command is available in all versions of Windows, as well as in MS-DOS.

167. Pentnt

    The pentnt command is used to detect floating point division errors in the Intel Pentium chip. The pentnt command is also used to enable floating point emulation and disable floating point hardware. The pentnt command is available in Windows XP. The pentnt command was removed beginning in Windows Vista due to the lack of Intel Pentium CPU use at the time of this operating system release.

168. Ping

The ping command sends an Internet Control Message Protocol (ICMP) Echo Request message to a specified remote computer to verify IP-level connectivity. The ping command is available in all versions of Windows.

169. Pkgmgr

The pkgmgr command is used to start the Windows Package Manager from the Command Prompt. Package Manager installs, uninstalls, configures, and updates features and packages for Windows. The pkgmgr command is available in Windows 10, Windows 8, Windows 7, and Windows Vista.

170. Pnpunattend

The pnpunattend command is used to automate the installation of hardware device drivers. The pnpunattend command is available in Windows 10, Windows 8, Windows 7, and Windows Vista.

171. Pnputil

The pnputil command is used to start the Microsoft PnP Utility, a tool used to install a Plug and Play device from the command line. The pnputil command is available in Windows 10, Windows 8, Windows 7, and Windows Vista.

172. Popd

The popd command is used to change the current directory to the one most recently stored by the pushd command. The popd command is most often utilized from within a batch or script file. The popd command is available in Windows 10, Windows 8, Windows 7, Windows Vista, and Windows XP.

173. Power

The power command is used to reduce the power consumed by a computer by monitoring software and hardware devices. The power command is available in Windows 98 and 95, as well as in MS-DOS. The power command was replaced by operating system integrated power management functions beginning in Windows XP.

174. Powercfg

    The powercfg command is used to manage the Windows power management settings from the command line. The powercfg command is available in Windows 10, Windows 8, Windows 7, Windows Vista, and Windows XP.

175. Print

    The print command is used to print a specified text file to a specified printing device. The print command is available in all versions of Windows, as well as in MS-DOS.

176. Prompt The prompt command is used to customize the appearance of the prompt text in Command Prompt or MS-DOS. The prompt command is available in all versions of Windows, as well as in MS-DOS.

177. Pushd

    The pushd command is used to store a directory for use, most commonly from within a batch or script program. The pushd command is available in Windows 10, Windows 8, Windows 7, Windows Vista, and Windows XP.

178. Pwlauncher

    The pwlauncher command is used to enable, disable, or show the status of your Windows To Go startup options. The pwlauncher command is available in Windows 10 and 8.

179. Qappsrv The qappsrv command is used to display all Remote Desktop Session Host servers available on the network. The qappsrv command is available in Windows 10, Windows 8, Windows 7, Windows Vista, and Windows XP.

180. Qbasic

    The qbasic command starts QBasic, the MS-DOS based programming environment for the BASIC programming language. The qbasic command is available in Windows 98 and 95, as well as in MS-DOS. The qbasic command is not installed by default with Windows 98 or 95 but is available from the installation disc or disks.

181. Qprocess

    The qprocess command is used to display information about

running processes. The qprocess command is available in Windows 10, Windows 8, Windows 7, Windows Vista, and Windows XP.

182. Query

The query command is used to display the status of a specified service. The query command is available in Windows 10, Windows 8, Windows 7, and Windows Vista.

183. Quser

The quser command is used to display information about users currently logged on to the system. The quser command is available in Windows 10, Windows 8, Windows 7, and Windows Vista.

184. Qwinsta

The qwinsta command is used to display information about open Remote Desktop Sessions. The qwinsta command is available in Windows 10, Windows 8, Windows 7, Windows Vista, and Windows XP.

185. Rasautou

The rasautou command is used to manage Remote Access Dialer AutoDial addresses. The rasautou command is available in Windows 10, Windows 8, Windows 7, Windows Vista, and Windows XP.

186. Rasdial

The rasdial command is used to start or end a network connection for a Microsoft client. The rasdial command is available in Windows 10, Windows 8, Windows 7, Windows Vista, and Windows XP.

187. Rcp

The rcp command is used to copy files between a Windows computer and a system running the rshd daemon. The rcp command is available in Windows 7, Windows Vista, and Windows XP. The rcp command is not available by default in Windows Vista or Windows 7 but can be enabled by turning on the Subsystem for UNIX-based Applications Windows feature from Programs and Features in Control Panel and then installing the Utilities and SDK for UNIX-based Applications available here for Windows Vista and here for Windows 7. The rcp command is not available in Windows 10 or 8 because Service for UNIX (SFU) was discontinued.

188. Rd

The rd command is the shorthand version of the rmdir command. The rd command is available in all versions of Windows, as well as in MS-DOS.

189. Rdpsign

The rdpsign command is used to sign a Remote Desktop Protocol (RDP) file. The rdpsign command is available in Windows 7.

190. Reagentc

The reagentc command is used to configure the Windows Recovery Environment (RE). The reagentc command is available in Windows 10, Windows 8, and Windows 7.

191. Recimg

The recimg command is used to create a custom refresh image. The recimg command is available in Windows 8.

192. Recover

The recover command is used to recover readable data from a bad or defective disk. The recover command is available in Windows 10, Windows 8, Windows 7, Windows Vista, and Windows XP.

193. Reg

The reg command is used to manage the Windows Registry from the command line. The reg command can perform common registry functions like adding registry keys, exporting the registry, etc. The reg command is available in Windows 10, Windows 8, Windows 7, Windows Vista, and Windows XP.

194. Regini

The regini command is used to set or change registry permissions and registry values from the command line. The regini command is available in Windows 10, Windows 8, Windows 7, Windows Vista, and Windows XP.

195. Register-cimprovider

    The register-cimprovider command is used to register a Common Information Model (CIM) Provider in Windows. The register-cimprovider command is available in Windows 10 and Windows 8.

196. Regsvr32

    The regsvr32 command is used to register a DLL file as a command component in the Windows Registry. The regsvr32 command is available in Windows 10, Windows 8, Windows 7, Windows Vista, and Windows XP.

197. Relog

    The relog command is used to create new performance logs from data in existing performance logs. The relog command is available in Windows 10, Windows 8, Windows 7, Windows Vista, and Windows XP.

198. Rem

    The rem command is used to record comments or remarks in a batch or script file. The rem command is available in all versions of Windows, as well as in MS-DOS.

199. Ren

    The ren command is the shorthand version of the rename command. The ren command is available in all versions of Windows, as well as in MS-DOS.

200. Rename

    The rename command is used to change the name of the individual file that you specify. The rename command is available in all versions of Windows, as well as in MS-DOS.

201. Repair-bde

    The repair-bde command is used to repair or decrypt a damaged drive that's been encrypted using BitLocker. The repair-bde command is available in Windows 10, Windows 8, and Windows 7.

202. Replace

    The replace command is used to replace one or more files with one or more other files. The replace command is available in all versions of Windows, as well as in MS-DOS.

203. Reset

The reset command, executed as reset session, is used to reset the session subsystem software and hardware to known initial values. The reset command is available in Windows 10, Windows 8, Windows 7, Windows Vista, and Windows XP.

204. Restore

The restore command is used to restore files that were backed up using the backup command. The restore command is only available in MS-DOS. The backup command was only available up to MS-DOS 5.00 but the restore command was included by default with later versions of MS-DOS to provide a way to restore files that were backed up in previous versions of MS-DOS.

205. Rexec

The rexec command is used to run commands on remote computers running the rexec daemon. The rexec command is available in Windows Vista and Windows XP. The rsh command is not available by default in Windows Vista but can be enabled by turning on the Subsystem for UNIX-based Applications Windows feature from Programs and Features in Control Panel and then installing the Utilities and SDK for UNIX-based Applications available here. The rexec command is not available in Windows 7 but can be executed in Windows XP via Windows XP Mode if need be.

206. Rmdir

The rmdir command is used to delete an existing or completely empty folder. The rmdir command is available in all versions of Windows, as well as in MS-DOS.

207. Robocopy

The robocopy command is used to copy files and directories from one location to another. This command is also called Robust File Copy. The robocopy command is available in Windows 10, Windows 8, Windows 7, and Windows Vista. The robocopy command is superior to both the copy command and the xcopy command because robocopy supports many more options.

208. Route

The route command is used to manipulate network routing tables. The route command is available in all versions of Windows.

209. Rpcinfo

The rpcinfo command makes a remote procedure call (RPC) to an RPC server and reports what it finds. The rpcinfo command is available in Windows 7 and Windows Vista. The rpcinfo command is not available by default in Windows Vista or Windows 7 but can be enabled by turning on the Services for NFS Windows feature from Programs and Features in Control Panel. The rpcinfo command is not available in Windows 8 because Service for UNIX (SFU) was discontinued.

210. Rpcping

The rpcping command is used to ping a server using RPC. The rpcping command is available in Windows 10, Windows 8, Windows 7, and Windows Vista.

211. Rsh

The rsh command is used to run commands on remote computers running the rsh daemon. The rsh command is available in Windows 7, Windows Vista, and Windows XP. The rsh command is not available by default in Windows Vista or Windows 7 but can be enabled by turning on the Subsystem for UNIX-based Applications Windows feature from Programs and Features in Control Panel and then installing the Utilities and SDK for UNIX-based Applications available here for Windows Vista and here for Windows 7. The rsh command is not available in Windows 10 or 8 because Service for UNIX (SFU) was discontinued.

212. Rsm

The rsm command is used to manage media resources using Removable Storage. The rsm command is available in Windows Vista and Windows XP. The rsm command was optional in

Windows Vista and then removed in Windows 7 due to Removable Storage Manager being removed from the operating system. Search for the rsm command in the C:\Windows\winsxs folder in Windows Vista if you're having trouble executing the command.

213. Runas

    The runas command is used to execute a program using another user's credentials. The runas command is available in Windows 10, Windows 8, Windows 7, Windows Vista, and Windows XP.

214. Rwinsta

    The rwinsta command is the shorthand version of the reset session command. The rwinsta command is available in Windows 10, Windows 8, Windows 7, Windows Vista, and Windows XP.

215. Sc

    The sc command is used to configure information about services. The sc command communicates with the Service Control Manager. The sc command is available in Windows 10, Windows 8, Windows 7, Windows Vista, and Windows XP.

216. Scandisk

    The scandisk command is used to start Microsoft ScanDisk, a disk repair program. The scandisk command is available in Windows 98 and 95, as well as in MS-DOS. The scandisk command was replaced by the chkdsk command beginning in Windows XP.

217. Scanreg

    The scanreg command starts Windows Registry Checker, a basic registry repair program and backup utility. The scanreg command is available in Windows 98 and Windows 95. The functions provided by the scanreg command were no longer necessary beginning in Windows XP due to changes in how the Windows Registry functions.

218. Schtasks

    The schtasks command is used to schedule specified programs or commands to run at certain times. The schtasks command can be used to create, delete, query, change, run, and end scheduled tasks. The schtasks command is available in Windows 10, Windows 8, Windows 7, Windows Vista, and Windows XP.

219. Sdbinst

The sdbinst command is used to deploy customized SDB database files. The sdbinst command is available in Windows 10, Windows 8, Windows 7, Windows Vista, and Windows XP.

220. Secedit

The secedit command is used to configure and analyze system security by comparing the current security configuration to a template. The secedit command is available in Windows 10, Windows 8, Windows 7, Windows Vista, and Windows XP.

221. Set

The set command is used to display, enable, or disable environment variables in MS-DOS or from the Command Prompt. The set command is available in all versions of Windows, as well as in MS-DOS.

222. Setlocal

The setlocal command is used to start the localization of environment changes inside a batch or script file. The setlocal command is available in Windows 10, Windows 8, Windows 7, Windows Vista, and Windows XP.

223. Setspn

The setspn command is used to manage the Service Principal Names (SPN) for an Active Directory (AD) service account. The setspn command is available in Windows 10, Windows 8, and Windows 7.

224. Setver

The setver command is used to set the MS-DOS version number that MS-DOS reports to a program. The setver command is available in MS-DOS as well as in all 32-bit versions of Windows. The setver command is not available in 64-bit versions of Windows.

225. Setx

The setx command is used to create or change environment

variables in the user environment or the system environment. The setx command is available in Windows 10, Windows 8, Windows 7, and Windows Vista.

226. Sfc

The sfc command is used to verify and replace important Windows system files. The sfc command is also referred to as System File Checker or Windows Resource Checker, depending on the operating system. The sfc command is available in Windows 10, Windows 8, Windows 7, Windows Vista, and Windows XP.

227. Shadow

The shadow command is used to monitor another Remote Desktop Services session. The shadow command is available in Windows 7, Windows Vista, and Windows XP.

228. Share

The share command is used to install file locking and file sharing functions in MS-DOS. The share command is available in MS-DOS as well as in all 32-bit versions of Windows. The share command is not available in 64-bit versions of Windows. Share is only available in Windows 10, 8, 7, Vista, and XP to support older MS-DOS files.

229. Shift

The shift command is used to change the position of replaceable parameters in a batch or script file. The shift command is available in all versions of Windows, as well as in MS-DOS.

230. Showmount

The showmount command is used to display information about NFS mounted file systems. The showmount command is available in Windows 7 and Windows Vista. The showmount command is not available by default in Windows Vista or Windows 7 but can be enabled by turning on the Services for NFS Windows feature from Programs and Features in Control Panel. The showmount command is not available in Windows 10 or 8 because Service for UNIX (SFU) was discontinued.

231. Shutdown

The shutdown command can be used to shut down, restart, or log off the current system or a remote computer. The shutdown command is available in Windows 10, Windows 8, Windows 7, Windows Vista, and Windows XP.

232. Smartdrv

The smartdrv command installs and configures SMARTDrive, a disk caching utility for MS-DOS. The smartdrv command is available in Windows 98 and 95, as well as in MS-DOS. Caching is automatic beginning in Windows XP, making the smartdrv command unnecessary.

233. Sort

The sort command is used to read data from a specified input, sort that data, and return the results of that sort to the Command Prompt screen, a file, or another output device. The sort command is available in all versions of Windows, as well as in MS-DOS.

234. Start

The start command is used to open a new command line window to run a specified program or command. The start command can also be used to start an application without creating a new window. The start command is available in all versions of Windows.

235. Subst

The subst command is used to associate a local path with a drive letter. The subst command is a lot like the net use command except a local path is used instead of a shared network path. The subst command is available in all versions of Windows, as well as in MS-DOS. The subst command replaced the assign command beginning with MS-DOS 6.0.

236. Sxstrace

The sxstrace command is used to start the WinSxs Tracing Utility, a programming diagnostic tool. The sxstrace command is available in Windows 10, Windows 8, Windows 7, and Windows Vista.

237. Sys

The sys command is used to copy the MS-DOS system files and command interpreter to a disk. The sys command is available in Windows 98 and 95, as well as in MS-DOS. The sys command is used most often to create a simple bootable disk or hard drive. The necessary system files for Windows are too large to fit on a disk, so the sys command was removed beginning in Windows XP.

238. Systeminfo

The systeminfo command is used to display basic Windows configuration information for the local or a remote computer. The systeminfo command is available in Windows 10, Windows 8, Windows 7, Windows Vista, and Windows XP.

239. Takeown

The takedown command is used to regain access to a file that that an administrator was denied access to when reassigning ownership of the file. The takeown command is available in Windows 10, Windows 8, Windows 7, and Windows Vista.

240. Taskkill

The taskkill command is used to terminate a running task. The taskkill command is the command line equivalent of ending a process in Task Manager in Windows. The taskkill command is available in Windows 10, Windows 8, Windows 7, Windows Vista, and Windows XP.

241. Tasklist

Displays a list of applications, services, and the Process ID (PID) currently running on either a local or a remote computer. The tasklist command is available in Windows 10, Windows 8, Windows 7, Windows Vista, and Windows XP.

242. Tcmsetup

The tcmsetup command is used to set up or disable the Telephony Application Programming Interface (TAPI) client. The tcmsetup command is available in Windows 10, Windows 8, Windows 7, Windows Vista, and Windows XP.

243. Telnet

The telnet command is used to communicate with remote computers that use the Telnet protocol. The telnet command is available in all versions of Windows. The telnet command is not available by default in Windows 10, 8, 7, or Vista, but can be enabled by turning on the Telnet Client Windows feature from Programs and Features in Control Panel.

244. Tftp

The tftp command is used to transfer files to and from a remote computer that's running the Trivial File Transfer Protocol (TFTP) service or daemon. The tftp command is available in Windows 10, Windows 8, Windows 7, Windows Vista, and Windows XP. The tftp command is not available by default in Windows 8, 7, or Vista, but can be enabled by turning on the TFTP Client Windows feature from Programs and Features in Control Panel.

245. Time

The time command is used to show or change the current time. The time command is available in all versions of Windows, as well as in MS-DOS.

246. Timeout

The timeout command is typically used in a batch or script file to provide a specified timeout value during a procedure. The timeout command can also be used to ignore keypresses. The timeout command is available in Windows 10, Windows 8, Windows 7, and Windows Vista.

247. Title

The title command is used to set the Command Prompt window title. The title command is available in Windows 10, Windows 8, Windows 7, Windows Vista, and Windows XP.

248. Tlntadmn

The tlntadmn command is used to administer a local or remote computer running Telnet Server. The tlntadmn command is available in Windows 10, Windows 8, Windows 7, Windows Vista, and Windows XP. The tlntadmn command is not available by default in Windows 8, 7, or Vista, but can be enabled by turning on the Telnet Server Windows feature from Programs and Features in Control Panel.

249. Tpmvscmgr

The tpmvscmgr command is used to create and destroy TPM virtual smart cards. The tpmvscmgr command is available in Windows 8.

250. Tracerpt

The tracerpt command is used to process event trace logs or real-time data from instrumented event trace providers. The tracerpt command is available in Windows 10, Windows 8, Windows 7, Windows Vista, and Windows XP.

251. Tracert

The tracert command sends Internet Control Message Protocol (ICMP) Echo Request messages to a specified remote computer with increasing Time to Live (TTL) field values and displays the IP address and hostname, if available, of the router interfaces between the source and destination. The tracert command is available in all versions of Windows.

252. Tree

The tree command is used to graphically display the folder structure of a specified drive or path. The tree command is available in all versions of Windows, as well as in MS-DOS.

253. Tscon

The tscon command is used to attach a user session to a Remote Desktop session. The tscon command is available in Windows 10, Windows 8, Windows 7, Windows Vista, and Windows XP.

254. Tsdiscon

The tsdiscon command is used to disconnect a Remote Desktop session. The tsdiscon command is available in Windows 10, Windows 8, Windows 7, Windows Vista, and Windows XP.

255. Tskill

The tskill command is used to end the specified process. The tskill command is available in Windows 10, Windows 8, Windows 7, Windows Vista, and Windows XP.

256. Tsshutdn

The tsshutdn command is used to remotely shut down or restart a terminal server. The tsshutdn command is available in Windows XP. The ability to shut down a computer remotely is also available in the more powerful shutdown command, so tsshutdn was removed beginning in Windows Vista.

257. Type

The type command is used to display the information contained in a text file. The type command is available in all versions of Windows, as well as in MS-DOS.

258. Typeperf

The typerperf command displays performance data in the Command Prompt window or writes the data to specified log file. The typeperf command is available in Windows 10, Windows 8, Windows 7, Windows Vista, and Windows XP.

259. Tzutil

The tzutil command is used to display or configure the current system's time zone. The tzutil command can also be used to enable or disable Daylight Saving Time adjustments. The tzutil command is available in Windows 10, Windows 8, and Windows 7.

260. Umount

The umount command is used to remove Network File System (NFS) mounted network shares. The umount command is available in Windows 7 and Windows Vista. The umount command is not available by default in Windows Vista or Windows 7 but can be enabled by turning on the Services for NFS Windows feature from Programs and Features in Control Panel. The umount command is not available in Windows 10 or 8 because Service for UNIX (SFU) was discontinued.

261. Undelete

The undelete command is used to undo a deletion performed with the MS-DOS delete command. The undelete command is only available in MS-DOS. The undelete command was removed beginning in Windows 95 due to the availability of the Recycle

Bin in Windows. Additionally, free file recovery programs are available from third-party software makers.

262. Unformat

The unformat command is used to undo the formatting on a drive performed by the MS-DOS format command. The unformat command is only available in MS-DOS. The unformat command was removed beginning in Windows 95 due to file system changes.

263. Unlock

The unlock command is used to unlock a drive, disabling direct disk access for a program. The unlock command is only available in Windows 98 and 95. Drive locking is no longer available as of Windows XP.

264. Unlodctr

The unlodctr command removes Explain text and Performance counter names for a service or device driver from the Windows Registry. The unlodctr command is available in Windows 10, Windows 8, Windows 7, Windows Vista, and Windows XP.

265. Vaultcmd

The vaultcmd command is used to create, remove, and show stored credentials. The vaultcmd command is available in Windows 10, Windows 8, and Windows 7.

266. Ver

The ver command is used to display the current Windows or MS-DOS version number. The ver command is available in all versions of Windows, as well as in MS-DOS.

267. Verify

The verify command is used to enable or disable the ability of Command Prompt, or MS-DOS, to verify that files are written correctly to a disk. The verify command is available in all versions of Windows, as well as in MS-DOS.

268. Vol

The vol command shows the volume label and serial number of a specified disk, assuming this information exists. The vol command is available in all versions of Windows, as well as in

MS-DOS.

269. **Vsafe**

The vsafe command is used to start VSafe, a basic virus protection system for MS-DOS. The vsafe command is only available in MS-DOS. VSafe was designed for MS-DOS and Windows 3.x only. Microsoft provides an optional virus protection suite called Microsoft Security Essentials for Windows XP and later operating systems, and third-party antivirus tools are available for all versions of Windows.

270. **Vssadmin**

The vssadmin command starts the Volume Shadow Copy Service administrative command line tool which displays current volume shadow copy backups and all installed shadow copy writers and providers. The vssadmin command is available in Windows 10, Windows 8, Windows 7, Windows Vista, and Windows XP.

271. **W32tm**

The w32tm command is used to diagnose issues with Windows Time. The w32tm command is available in Windows 10, Windows 8, Windows 7, Windows Vista, and Windows XP.

272. **Waitfor**

The waitfor command is used to send or wait for a signal on a system. The waitfor command is available in Windows 10, Windows 8, Windows 7, and Windows Vista.

273. **Wbadmin**

The wbadmin command is used to start and stop backup jobs, display details about a previous backup, list the items within a backup, and report on the status of a currently running backup. The wbadmin command is available in Windows 10, Windows 8, Windows 7, and Windows Vista. The wbadmin command replaced the ntbackup command beginning in Windows Vista.

274. **Wecutil**

The wecutil command is used to manage subscriptions to events that are forwarded from WS-Management supported computers. The wecutil command is available in Windows 10, Windows 8,

Windows 7, and Windows Vista.

275. Wevtutil

The wevtutil command starts the Windows Events Command Line Utility which is used to manage event logs and publishers. The wevtutil command is available in Windows 10, Windows 8, Windows 7, and Windows Vista.

276. Where

The where command is used to search for files that match a specified pattern. The where command is available in Windows 10, Windows 8, Windows 7, and Windows Vista.

277. Whoami

The whoami command is used to retrieve user name and group information on a network. The whoami command is available in Windows 10, Windows 8, Windows 7, and Windows Vista.

278. Winmgmt

The winmgmt command starts the command line version of WMI, a scripting tool in Windows. The winmgmt command is available in all versions of Windows.

279. Winrm

The winrm command is used to start the command line version of Windows Remote Management, used to manage secure communications with local and remote computers using web services. The winrm command is available in Windows 10, Windows 8, Windows 7, and Windows Vista.

280. Winrs

The winrs command is used to open a secure command window with a remote host. The winrs command is available in Windows 10, Windows 8, Windows 7, and Windows Vista.

281. Winsat

The winsat command starts the Windows System Assessment Tool, a program that assesses various features, attributes, and capabilities of a computer running Windows. The winsat command is available in Windows 10, Windows 8, Windows 7, and Windows Vista.

282. Wmic

The wmic command starts the Windows Management Instrumentation Command line (WMIC), a scripting interface that simplifies the use of Windows Management Instrumentation (WMI) and systems managed via WMI. The wmic command is available in Windows 10, Windows 8, Windows 7, Windows Vista, and Windows XP.

283. Wsmanhttpconfig

The wsmanhttpconfig command is used to manage aspects of the Windows Remote Management (WinRM) service. The wsmanhttpconfig command is available in Windows 10, Windows 8, Windows 7, and Windows Vista.

284. Xcopy

The xcopy command can copy one or more files or directory trees from one location to another. The xcopy command is generally considered a more "powerful" version of the copy command through the robocopy command trumps even xcopy. The xcopy command is available in all versions of Windows, as well as in MS-DOS. A command by the name of xcopy32 existed in Windows 95 and Windows 98. To avoid a long and confusing explanation here, just know that no matter if you executed the xcopy command or the xcopy32 command, you were always executing the most updated version of the command.

285. Xwizard

The xwizard command, short for Extensible Wizard, is used to register data in Windows, often from a preconfigured XML file. The xwizard command is available in Windows 10, Windows 8, and Windows 7.

www.ingramcontent.com/pod-product-compliance
Lightning Source LLC
LaVergne TN
LVHW012035060526
838201LV00061B/4622